FORGIVENESS & REPENTANCE

A DEVOTIONAL JOURNAL

By

PAMELA TUCKER

Copyright © 2020 by Pamela Tucker

All rights reserved.

Printed in the United States of America

First Printing, 2020

ISBN: 978-1-7350031-5-3

Email: restartenterprise2017@gmail.com

All scripture references are taken from the King James Version unless otherwise stated.

Day One

Forbearing and Forgiving

Forbearing one another, and forgiving one another, if any man have quarrel against any: even as Christ forgave you, so also do ye.

Colossians 3:13

The text focuses on forgiveness, in dealing with people, whether at work, home and in the world at large, misunderstandings and offences are inevitable. It is the duty of a Christian to forgive and forbear like our Savior Jesus Christ. The two virtues are not cheap but you can get it from the Holy Spirit when you are born again. "Forgiveness is so difficult because that devil embeds forth all his attempts to grip the memory of the pain there, lest we should forgive each other. However, there is always excellent help available from the Holy Spirit, and that help is sufficient for every such need."To forbear is to be patient with someone who wronged you, dismissing every vengeful feeling that may come up. Forgiveness entails letting go of past offences as though they never happened and treating the offender with love. Remember, love's influence to forgive is greater than hatred's influence for vengeance.

Jesus Christ forgave us freely, entirely and forever. He gives power to love, forbear and forgive; receive Him.

Day Two

Your Thoughts On

Forbearing and Forgiving

Day Three

The Call For Forgiveness

¹⁸And the LORD drave out from before us all the people, even the Amorites which dwelt in the land: [therefore] will we also serve the LORD; for he [is] our God.

¹⁹And Joshua said unto the people, Ye cannot serve the LORD: for he [is] an holy God; he [is] a jealous God; he will not forgive your transgressions nor your sins.

Joshua 24 :19

Martin Luther said, "Forgiveness is God's command." Though we may agree that forgiveness is a central principle of Christianity and many times, we find it difficult to forgive those who have hurt us. And a lot of times such offences could be very insignificant and not worth grudging about but we just choose not to let go and forgive others. As a believer, we must learn to forgive and forget, though we might struggle to practice it at first but if we are deliberate about it we will build a forgiving spirit over time. Forgiveness is a gift we freely receive from God and a gift we must freely give.

In our text, the people of Israel were asked whether they would choose to serve God as they had made their way out from the land of Egypt into the Promised Land. Joshua, the servant of the Lord, admonished the children of Israel to "Choose for yourselves this day whom you will serve. . . . But as for me and my household, we will serve the LORD" (v. 15).

Unfortunately, the children of Israel got offended by Joshua's admonition. But Joshua reminded the people of Israel about God's loving character. They serve a God who will not tolerate partial allegiance. He is both "Holy" and "jealous" (v. 19). The word "forgive" in our text means to "bear with" or "live with".

Therefore, if we neglect the call to forgive those who offend us, our heavenly Father will not forgive us of our sins. If we do not show compassion to others, it will invariable affect our Christian faith.

Day Four

Your Thoughts On

The Call For Forgiveness

Day Five

Forgiveness is The Cure

O Israel Do not fear, for I have redeemed you; I have called thee by thy name; you are mine.

Isaiah 43 : 1

In a study, results shows that people who are forgiving tend to have not only less stress but also better relationships, a little general health problem and lower incidences of heart disease stroke and cancer

Today's text reveals the magnitude of God's love for His people, despite their dis-obedient attitude. Instead of God rejecting and neglecting them in anger, He still offers inestimable love. God's endless love for his people shows his sovereignty to forgive us from all our trespasses.

Amazingly, God's people see the verses as a love poem. God reaffirms His care and love: "I will be with you" (vs. 2); "I have loved thee" (vs. 4). We are highly treasured as God's creature (vs. 7). God has unlimited power to save His people (vs. 11–13).

He allows us to seek forgiveness in His love. Despite the efficacy of God's provision and salvation, they have disappointed and disobeyed their Redeemer (vs. 14–22).

God offers us hope and forgiveness "I, even I, am he that blotteth out thy transgressions for mine own sake, and will not remember thy sins" (vs. 25).

We forgive to be forgiven. Forgiveness is offered, because He loves us and it delights Him to redeem us.

Day Six

Your Thoughts On

Forgiveness is The Cure

Day Seven

Consequence of Unforgiveness Towards Others

And forgive us our debts, as we forgive our debtors.

Matthew 6:12

Perhaps you remember an old school mate who trampled and bullied you. Or you might recall a family member who failed to keep a promise. Maybe you were treated unfairly by your employer or cheated when making a purchase. Most of us could easily remember the way others have treated us in a negative way.

The text warns us against hypocrisy in prayer. Jesus instructs us not to be like people who stand "for they love to pray standing in the synagogues and in the corners of the streets, that they may be seen of men" (vs. 5). We are to pray in sincerity and not to be carried away with the length of our prayers.

Jesus teaches His disciples on how to pray. The Lord's Prayer has been used in worship, sermons and it has been a blessing to believers. It contains adoration for God's supremacy, confession for sins, acknowledgment of His holiness, and a supplication for guidance and protection.

But with our attention on forgiveness, notice how Christ's prayer emphasizes its necessity: "For if you forgive men their trespasses, your heavenly Father will also forgive you" (v. 14).

This is a promise from our creator. Someone said, "I honestly won't forgive someone for hurting me because forgiving someone for their mistakes is like accepting them to do it again." When we forgive others, closing the account of their wrong deeds from our mind, our hearts are open to experience God's forgiveness.

If we fail to forgive another, there will be mental, emotional and physical disorder and much stress. "But if ye forgive not men their trespasses, neither will your Father forgive your trespasses" (vs. 15). Our willingness to forgive reveals our closeness with the Lord.

Day Eight

Your Thoughts On

Consequence of Unforgiveness Towards Others

Day Nine

The Gift Of Forgiveness

Hearken therefore unto the supplications of thy servant, and of thy people Israel, which they shall make toward this place: hear thou from thy dwelling place, [even] from heaven; and when thou hearest, forgive.

2 Chronicles 6:21

To be totally forgiven is indeed a surprising gift, packaged for us by God Himself. Today's passage records Solomon's prayer of dedication for the temple. He knelt, with his hands raised toward heaven, and communed with God: "There is no God like thee in heaven, nor in the earth" (v. 14). He appreciated God's greatness, and declared that this earthly temple no matter how grand cannot contain thee (vs. 18).

Recognizing the exalted nature of God and the earthly nature of God's people, Solomon asked that God hear their prayers and when He hears their confessions, that He would forgive them (v. 21). Notice how often Solomon makes the plea in these verses: "hear from heaven and forgive" (vs. 30). No matter maybe the challenge and difficulty of God's people, they must turn to the Lord and plead for His forgiveness.

God doesn't joke with sin, but He also offers the gift of forgiveness. This gift of forgiveness is not for the purpose of continuing in sin; rather, forgiveness gives us the manifold blessing of being able to follow God and serve Him with all our heart. "Forgive, and deal with everyone according to all they do, since you know their hearts (for you alone know the human heart), so that they will fear you and walk in obedience to you" (vv. 30–31).

Forgive, and render unto every man according unto all his ways, whose heart thou knowest; (for thou only knowest the hearts of the children of men), that they may hear thee, to walk in thy ways , so long as they live in the land which thou gavest unto our fathers.

Day Ten

Your Thoughts On

The Gift Of Forgiveness

Day Eleven

Love Your Neighbour

And the second is like, namely this, Thou shalt love thy neighbor as thyself. There is none other commandment greater than these.

Mark 12:31

A dictionary defines neighbor as "a person who lives near another". This is the general definition of his word. However, Christ's definition of a neighbor is quite different and quite extensive. Therefore, when the Bible talks about neighbors, it is talking about humanity in general. God is Love, and expects His children to love others as well. All your coworkers or people in the street are your neighbors and deserve your love irrespective of their attitude towards you and the gospel. You can be of help to fellow colleagues when they are in need that you can provide solutions to.

The greatest help you can render to your neighbor is to open their eyes to the saving truth of the Bible. Many are ignorant of the judgment that is about to befall the world because of sin. It is love that brought you into the kingdom, so you must allow the same love to constrain you to bring others to God too. The Good Samaritan showed love to his neighbor who was wounded.

Day Twelve

Your Thoughts On

Love Your Neighbour

Day Thirteen

Forgive us as we Forgive Others

And forgive us our sins; for we also forgive everyone that is indebted to us. And lead us not into temptation, but deliver us from evil.

Luke 11:4

The world and the human race are designed in such a way that man can interact with other men. This can be directly or indirectly, physically or not physically; Man engages in interactions and transactions with each other daily and even momentarily, as time and opportunities avail them.

Subsequently, actions may inevitably lead to an offense, and when offenses are not rightly approached, it will surely lead to unforgiveness. The scriptures, on different occasions and in various teachings admonish us on how to live happily, joyful and healthily.

One of the healthy measures of living is forgiveness. A man who lives all his life full of unforgiveness has successfully robbed himself of joy, happiness, excitement and all the fun that life offers him; just because of unforgiveness.

An aged man once lived and one of his sons asked him what he desired to advise him on. The aged man spoke cheerfully and said, 'I could live as long as I have lived and be happy everyday because of what I call a forgiveness diet'. He further explained that forgiveness should be a daily diet that man should take. And this is a 'truth diet' indeed.

Could it be that many live in bitterness, hatred, anger, regret and shortens their life just because of unforgiveness? Though, many live longer but stay moody, embittered, hateful, depressed, and hostile because they refuse to forgive an offense. Many have refused to go into another relationship; contractual or marital because of unforgiveness. The consequences of unforgiveness are numerous and you know what it has caused, denied and robbed you off as well.

You can cheerfully live your life when you take a daily diet of forgiveness. 'Let not the sunset on your anger', the scripture admonishes. So, never go to bed while you still hold an offense at work, in office, at home, in the church or anywhere to heart, against any person. Take your daily diet of forgiveness.

Day Fourteen

Your Thoughts On

Forgive us as we Forgive Others

Day Fifteen

How Many Times Should I Forgive My Brother ?

Even if they sin against you seven times in a day to you saying 'i repent ; you must forgive them ".

Luke 17 : 4

Forgiveness is a powerful force that allows us to let go of resentment, anger, bitterness, hatred, jealousy and so much more, But why do people feel that they should not forgive a person/people more than once? Do we only ask God to forgive us only one time? I do understand it can be hard to forgive a person/people for the same action over and over again. Though you can justify your feelings of hatred, anger, even frustration for that person or people that have wronged you. Let me ask you a question, holding them in a place of unforgiveness where does that place you? How much influence do they hold over you that you can't forgive? Who are you holding in the prison of your mind that you need to let them go free and forgive them? Not only are you freeing them from your mind and heart but you are freeing yourself from a jail with no bars that you held yourself in too long. Forgive and Be Free.

Day Sixteen

Your Thoughts On

How Many Times Should I Forgive My Brother?

Day Seventeen

Forgive Quickly

Then said Jesus, Father, forgive them; for they know not what they do.

Luke 23:34

We sometimes hold on to a situation that causes us pain and disappointment from others. We allow the emotions of the hurt to linger too long.

We have to learn how to Forgive quickly without holding on to resentment,bitterness, wrath, envy, and even anger.

We have to realize that the longer we wait to Forgive, the more time the enemy has to add salt to the wound and, we all know that does not feel good.

Sometimes people do things without thinking and understanding the process of their words or actions .

However, if you need an example to forgive quickly think about Jesus when he was hanging on the cross, what did he say?

Father forgive them for they know not what they do. Jesus did not wait to ask the FATHER to Forgive them.

Day Eighteen

Your Thoughts On

Forgive Quickly

_____
_____
_____
_____
_____
_____
_____
_____
_____
_____
_____
_____
_____
_____
_____
_____
_____
_____
_____

Day Nineteen

Forgiveness Brings Blessings

Blessed is the one whose transgressions are forgiven, whose sins are covered. Blessed is the one whose sin the Lord does not count against them and in whose spirit is no deceit

Psalms 32:1-2

Did you know that forgiveness can bring blessings? forgiveness can result in exceptional blessings for you and others. So many times we hold back our blessings because we choose not to forgive, we choose to think that if we hold on to that hatred or that resentment even abuse or misuse that somehow or another is going to keep that person in that situation it does not keep a person in a situation, it keeps you in a place that

I call a jail without bars. You confined yourself to an area of the memory of your mind.

You hold yourself to the memories and into the events of what had happened or taking place in your life that was not good for you at that time but understand where you are now that you realize that you need to forgive not only those that hurt you but yourself. You realize that Forgiveness Brings Blessings.

God forgives us through the blood of Jesus Christ. That is a blessing, That Jesus would shed His blood for the human race that would accept Him and believe in Him that we may not be lost.

Jesus paid the price, a ransom for us that is a blessing.

Forgiveness Brings Blessings Don't Miss Yours.

Day Twenty

Your Thoughts On

Forgiveness Brings Blessings

Day Twenty One

How Does it Feel to Forgive

Here is a question for you.

Have you ever thought that you had forgiven someone then God tells you that you haven't ?

One day in prayer God said you have not forgiven that person that hurt you. I was crushed to hear God say that to me. I know that I had been avoiding that person all that time. Even though I said I had forgiven him. Trying not to be at the same place with him was getting hard to do. We attended the same church. I would go to the early morning service, and he would go to the 11 am service. One day he showed up to the early morning service after the service, I had a meeting. I was trying my best to get out of there, but I could leave just yet. Next thing I know here he comes. Hey I haven't seen you in a while with a big grin on his face.I was very short with my words he caught the message after a few moments and he left. I felt bad I asked God to help me to forgive him. Sometimes it is hard to forgive people who think they don't have to apologize for their mistakes, but with

God leading and guiding you can do it. I truly forgiven him, not just saying I forgive you but, I truly forgave that person with my mouth and my heart. I felt agape love for that person.

When I tell you that God did that and it was one of the best things that could ever happen to me, the weight that I was carrying was gone. I felt so light my shoulders got light. I felt free.

Day Twenty Two

Your Thoughts On

How Does it Feel to Forgive

Day Twenty Three

Forgiveness is Freedom

If we confess our sins, he is faithful and just to forgive us our sins, and to cleanse us from all unrighteousness

1 John 1:9

Any person can be carrying hostility, but it takes a person with integrity and great character to forgive others.

When you forgive others, you are liberating yourself from a painful, depressing burden off life.

Forgiveness does not indicate what transpired was okay furthermore, it doesn't mean that person should still be allowed in your life again.

It just means you have made peace with the hurt and pain of it all, and you are willing to let it go.

Is there anyone in your life that you need to forgive?

It is freedom in forgiveness.

Day Twenty Four

Your Thoughts On

Forgiveness is Freedom

Day Twenty Five

Forgive Yourself

Therefore, I tell you, her many sins have been forgiven—as her great love has shown. But whoever has been forgiven little loves little."Then Jesus said to her, "Your sins are forgiven."The other guests began to say among themselves, "Who is this who even forgives sins?" Jesus said to the woman, "Your faith has saved you; go in peace.

Luke 7: 47-50

When we go through this journey of life and sometimes it is hard to let go of all the Ism and ism of our mind. As you move forward take some time to forgive yourself. Don't hold yourself in the prison of your mind, let yourself go and be free to laugh, sing to dance and to love it is imperative that you take a look at your life in every area. Be honest with yourself and if it's any area you need to forgive yourself, give yourself permission to be forgiven.

So many people go through life forgiving others but never take the time to forgive themselves. They hate themselves for different reasons don't do yourself like that. You forgive others but you are bound up with bitterness, envy, and even hatred toward yourself.

Stop tearing yourself up with negative words.

Speak positive words over your life that will build you up into the greatness that God has for you. You are God's masterpiece and He loves you.

Day Twenty Six

Your Thoughts On

Forgive Yourself

Day Twenty Seven

True Repentance

If my people, which are called by my name, shall humble themselves, and pray, and seek my face, and turn from their wicked ways; then will I hear from heaven, and will forgive their sin, and will heal their land.

2 chronicles 7:14

A lot of time, certain words seem easier to say or teach rather than being done. Repentance is one of those acts we found difficult to do but easier to teach or tell others to do. People become sober, humble and serious about repentance, they cry and promise a turnaround, they indeed want to leave that old life and desire to live a new life, but after a little while, they unconsciously get back to their previous ways. Repentance is not just about momentary humility, sorry, or guilt about a bad act, it involves an unbending and conscious decision to discontinue every unlawful and sinful act. It brings about a genuine and total transformation of a person, from being bad to good, from unrighteous to righteous, from darkness to light and from sin to salvation. However, true repentance does not just come by all those mere decisions; it requires subsequent observation and guidance towards the maintenance of the new life, lest we are found slipping into the old ways.

A beautiful thing about true repentance is the victory that follows. Everyone who truly repented always becomes better, and most importantly becomes useful to the kingdom of God. You are no more in the secret pattern of living like you used to be; a life of 'hide and seek'. Now, you have come into the light, whereby you walk with clarity and vision in the knowledge and will of God. Apart from the individual victory it brings to you, there is victory also in the kingdom of God; victory over the kingdom of darkness for a soul saved.

I say unto you, that likewise joy shall be in heaven over one sinner that repenteth, more than over ninety and nine just persons, which need no repentance.

Luke 15:7

True repentance under a scriptural definition can be summarized under two categories. In the first place, repentance is a total act of forsaking all self-misleading acts. Second, atonement requires humbling yourself to acknowledge the scriptural prosecution of your transgression, the scriptural charge regarding your wrongdoing, and the scriptural pathway to triumph over your transgression.

¹¹For godly sorrow worketh repentance to salvation not to be repented of: but the sorrow of the world worketh death. 12 For behold this self same thing, that ye sorrowed after a godly sort, what carefulness it wrought in you, yea, [what] clearing of yourselves, yea, [what] indignation, yea, [what] fear, yea, [what] vehement desire, yea, [what] zeal, yea, [what] revenge! In all [things] ye have approved yourselves to be clear in this matter.

2 Corinthians 7:11-12

Day Twenty Eight

Your Thoughts On

True Repentance

_____
_____
_____
_____
_____
_____
_____
_____
_____
_____
_____
_____
_____
_____
_____
_____
_____
_____
_____
_____

Day Twenty Nine

Mere Repentance
and True Repentance

²⁹*And it came to pass, that at midnight the LORD smote all the firstborn in the land of Egypt, from the firstborn of Pharaoh that sat on his throne unto the firstborn of the captive that [was] in the dungeon; and all the firstborn of cattle. 30 And Pharaoh rose up in the night, he, and all his servants, and all the Egyptians; and there was a great cry in Egypt; for [there was] not a house where [there was] not one dead.*

³¹*And he called for Moses and Aaron by night, and said, Rise up, [and] get you forth from among my people, both ye and the children of Israel; and go, serve the LORD, as ye have said.*

Exodus 12:29

There are specific examples in the word of God regarding people who sought forgiveness and repentance but did not truly repent. They were sorry, they regretted their sinful act and confessed their sins but never exercised true repentance. People like Esau, Balaam, Judas, and Saul. (In Exodus 12:29–32, Numbers 22:32–35, Matthew 27:7, Hebrews 12:17…)

The situation of Esau was described in one verse of the scripture, in Hebrews 12:17, F or ye know how that afterward, when he would have inherited the blessing, he was rejected: for he found no place of repentance, though he sought it carefully with tears. Just like Balaam and Pharaoh, Esau's heart was not indeed broken over his sins, he was not deeply sorry for the discomfort he had caused or the sin he had committed against the will of God. His core reason for repentance was for the things, which are materialistic that he wanted to regain. He was only sorry for the inheritance he needed to reclaim and not for the sake of his integrity or redemption in the sight of God. What a selfish apology! We see in the case of Balaam as well;

32 And the angel of the LORD said unto him, Wherefore hast thou smitten thine ass these three times? behold, I went out to withstand thee, because [thy] way is perverse before me:

33 And the ass saw me, and turned from me these three times: unless she had turned from me, surely now also I had slain thee, and saved her alive.

[34]And Balaam said unto the angel of the LORD, I have sinned; for I knew not that thou stoodest in the way against me: now therefore, if it displease thee, I will get me back again.

[35]And the angel of the LORD said unto Balaam, Go with the men: but only the word that I shall speak unto thee, that thou shalt speak. So Balaam went with the princes of Balak.

Number 22:32-35

God sees our heart, He sees our intent for every action we take and He responds more to our motive rather than our words or actions. Any repentance that is forged by selfish intent is false. Mere repentance focuses on the consequences attached to an error or sin you have committed rather than the sin itself. Your desires to receive earthly reward should never be the reason to take a turn for repentance, and even if you do, seek for true repentance, God is interested in that.

The world is governed by principles of reaping what is sown. The consequence of every sin is definitely unshakable or removable. However, when we run to Jesus, He cleanses us and redeems us to Himself. His redemptive power comes with a package of blessing and power; Blessings and power to walk through the consequences. There are some ways to know or identify true repentance, first, when your repentance is channeled towards the true will of God; knowing you've sinned and indeed gone against the will of the father. He loves us dearly, undoubtedly, and that moment we feel remorseful for betraying His love. Another way is to honestly confess a particular sin we have committed. This is not about merely stating your sins as a mistake; you take responsibility and deeply accept you consciously sinned. Also, true repentance demands that you turn away totally from that unrighteous path to the righteous path of God. It is the decision never to go back to the old sinful nature you have forsaken. True repentance cannot happen if there is no significant transformation in life. And on the other hand, mere repentance is characterized by selfish intentions and desires to receive the response of God for a certain situation and not for His love. it focuses on avoiding the consequences and punishment attached to sin. And rather than taking responsibility for the wrong deeds, it simply makes you shift blames and attach the cause to something or someone else.

Day Twenty Thirty

Your Thoughts On

Mere Repentance and True Repentance

Day Thirty One

Repentance and Forgiveness

¹⁶Then Pharaoh called for Moses and Aaron in haste; and he said, I have sinned against the LORD your God, and against you.

¹⁷Now therefore forgive, I pray thee, my sin only this once, and entreat the LORD your God, that he may take away from me this death only.

¹⁸And he went out from Pharaoh, and entreated the LORD.

¹⁹And the LORD turned a mighty strong west wind, which took away the locusts, and cast them into the Red sea; there remained not one locust in all the coasts of Egypt.

Exodus 10:16-19

Obviously, an average new believer seeks forgiveness more than repentance. Asking for forgiveness of sin is simply the first step to salvation and it is not a sufficient condition on its own. The true step to salvation is repentance. However, we often sidestep or rather do not treat repentance vividly as a new believer. Especially when we find ourselves in a challenging situation and all we need to move on at that time is God, we become so humble in God's presence and just expect God to give us His attention. The work of transformation from a sinful life to a life in Christ is not limited to the confession of sins and the request for its forgiveness. Those are very important, and as well basic. Nevertheless, all of those must be followed by a changed life; a sincere and intentional change that is beyond that present moment of humility, guilt, and reflections.

You remember the story of Pharaoh and Moses. Pharaoh was so adamant and he refused to let the Israelite go in accordance with the word of God. God began to fight Egypt with numerous plagues, which were felt all over their territory, yet Pharaoh would not let them go. He had his decision and was deliberate about it. And the Lord further sent plagues which destroyed all herbs and also sent the death angel to kill their firstborn. That seems huge and humbling. Pharaoh was forced to seek forgiveness. Evidently, Pharaoh never repentant from his desperate intention, he only went to God for the sake of his land to be restored, and his disobedience destroyed him. Seeking for forgiveness intermittently is not the plan and intention of God for us. It simply shows we are not ready to walk with God. It implies we are not ready to totally forsake our wrong ways. And what good does that do? Of course, no good! It only brings us back to a moment of regret and failure. Our lives keep revolving around the formal bad paths we have been treading. Only if we can repent, I mean 'repent' in its true meaning then our lives can experience a change and better living.

Remember Saul too?

Day Thirty Two

Your Thoughts On

Repentance and Forgiveness

Day Thirty Three

Repentance and Guilt

³Then Judas, which had betrayeth him, when he saw that he was condemned, repented himself, and brought again the thirty pieces of silver to the chief priests and elders,

⁴Saying, I have sinned in that I have betrayed the innocent blood. And they said, What [is that] to us? see thou [to that.]

⁵And he cast down the pieces of silver in the temple, and departed, and went and hanged himself.

Matthew 27:3-5

Our redemption in Christ is a complete work of salvation. Our reception is not partial, Jesus paid completely. And at any time we come to Him, with a sincere heart of repentance, He forgives and purifies us wholly and gives us a new mind like His (Let this mind be in you, which was also in Christ Jesus. Philippians 2:5). We receive a new mind that is free from unrighteousness and our old sinful nature. We do not have to worry or remember our old ways. Just in a moment, in the twinkle of an eye, and at the very moment we call on Him, Jesus, for forgiveness and purification, He washes us clean and totally wipes away our sins. If only we can spiritually look into His records, we would see Him erase our sins.

Clearly, we have no reason to feel guilty or allow our minds to revolve around occurrences and activities of our old ways. You do not necessarily have to feel regret for those things you cannot recover. Such regret will only set you back into the same consciousness of that sin and could result in life condemnation. You have no regrets with regard to what was necessary to produce the repentance in your life. You look at the circumstances it took for you to see your sin rightly and finally turn from them, and you see them as great blessings from God because they resulted in freeing your soul from its bondage to sin. Based on this definition, you are not truly repentant if you are picking apart the process by which sin is exposed, railing against the consequences of sin being exposed, or self-pitying in the fallout from sin being exposed.

Can we think about Judas for a while? Did he ever repent or seek for forgiveness? Yes, he repented but never allowed his mind to be renewed. He returned the money, which was given for betraying Jesus, but never truly renewed his mind. The central effect of every sin is on the mind and it places a destructive set of thinking in the human consciousness. Despite the fact that Judas repented, he still hung himself.

How many of us still live this way? Do you still allow your sins to deprive you of your inheritance and glorious privileges in Christ? **The NIV version of Act chapter 3 verse 19 says, "repent, then, and turn to God, so that your sins may be wiped out, that times of refreshing may come from the Lord."** Our repentance must be characterized with an honest turning towards God. There must be a significant mind transformation to a new life in Christ. Be deliberate in your decisions, let your determination to change be well emphasized even more than your quickness to ask for forgiveness. Remember, whoever hides his sin shall not prosper and God is so merciful towards everyone who's to Him.

For if ye turn again unto the LORD, your brethren and your children [shall find] compassion before them that lead them captive, so that they shall come again into this land: for the LORD your God [is] gracious and merciful, and will not turn away [his] face from you, if ye return unto him.

2 Chronicles 30:9

Day Thirty Four

Your Thoughts On

Repentance and Guilt

www.ingramcontent.com/pod-product-compliance
Lightning Source LLC
Chambersburg PA
CBHW032218040426
42449CB00005B/657